THE AUTHORS

Luca Stefano Cristini has edited various publications on ancient and contemporary historical themes, including books on thirty years war, Medieval, Napoleonic as well as several illustrated books with historical color photographs. He has also curated all the brands of Soldiershop publishing.

Joel Bellviure is a young Spanish historical researcher. He is particularly interested in early color photography techniques, colourisation, and History. He is currently studying History at the University of Barcelona. He is also the creator of Cassowary Colorizations.

Roberto Costanzo was born in 1963, lives near Novara in Italy. he is a passionate about history, modeling and graphic art. Roberto trying to make current photographs of a hundred years ago so that "we can see what they saw". He work at his project from 2014 and make specific research and improve some new technique. Publishes under the pseudonym ROCOlor. It's his first editorial experience with Soldiershop.

Anna Cristini born in 1992, lives and works in Spain. Daughter of the publisher Luca Cristini, despite his young age, has already done a lot of experience in the field of editorial illustration

PUBLISHING'S NOTES

LICENSES COMMONS

ACKNOWLEDGEMENTS

A Special Thanks to our friend Flynn Harris, and also to National Library of Scotland for his policy of free use of his WW1 images. Thanks to the Europeana Collections, and at all the several institution, museum, library, bibliotecks, public or private collection & athenaeums that with their positive copyright policy about part of his collections, allows us the use of many images present in our books. We remember same of this great World Institutions: New York Public Library, Rara CH, Heidelberg Biblioteck University, US Library of Congress, Riikmuseum of Amsterdam, Dusseldorf University Library, Polona Library, Herzog August Bibliothek of Wolfenbüttel, Stuttgart Bibliothek, SLUB Dresden, Frankfurt am Main Universitätsbibliothek, Europeana, Wikipedia, and many others...

Title: **ENGLISH, CANADIAN, ANZAC & INDIAN ARMIES IN THE GREAT WAR** - I soldati dell'impero britannico nella Grande Guerra
By Luca Stefano Cristini, Joel Bellviure, Roberto Costanzo e Anna Cristini.
ISBN code: 978-88-93273411First edition May 2018
Code.: **WW1-005**

Cover & Art Design: Luca S. Cristini
WW1&2 brand is a trademark of Soldiershop Publishing, via Padre Davide, 7 - 24050 Zanica (BG) ITALY.

ENGLISH, CANADIAN, ANZAC & INDIAN ARMIES IN THE GREAT WAR

I SOLDATI DELL'IMPERO BRITANNICO NELLA GRANDE GUERRA

BY LUCA STEFANO CRISTINI, JOEL BELLVIURE,
ROBERTO COSTANZO & ANNA CRISTINI

SOLDIERSHOP PUBLISHING

BOOKS TO COLLECT

THE GREAT WAR IN COLOUR

EXTRAORDINARY COLOURISED IMAGES BRING TO LIFE THE HORRORS FACING BY THE SOLDIERS DURING THE FIRST WORLD WAR

When you look at old black and white photos, the past seems very far away. This is especially apparent with First World War photographs. Soldiershop is proud to present in the 100th anniversary of the end of the First World War his project of colorized images of the WW1, The images featured not only the great battles of the war, but also life on the home front, wartime industries, the hospitals, the advances in the field of technology and communications ...

The Great War in Colour project will consist of colourizing of several of the better images about the year 1914-1918 from various Library and Archives of the world.

A Special Thanks to the several institution, museum, library, bibliotecks, public or private collection & athenaeums that with their positive copyright policy about part of his collections, allows us the use of many images present in our books realized for the centennial of the Armistice.

Several million black-and-white photos exist in the world's archives of events during the First World War, captured in myriad photographs on all sides of the front. Most of this photos show the devastating events of the Great War were.

Since then, a lot of books of black-and-white photographs of the war have been published as all nations endeavour to comprehend the scale and the carnage of the "terrible war of the 20th century". To mark the centenary of the outbreak of war, our books brings together all of these remarkable, fully recolored images of WW1.

The volume represents the work of several artists and collaborators of Soldiershop, but especially it is based on the work of the authors: Luca Cristini, Joel Bellviure, Roberto Costanzo and Anna Cristini

Our book presents all the text of the plates in English and Italian language.

◄ 1914, Daddy's escort. The delivery for the Europe of the first Tommies soldiers.

1914, Il papà va alla guerra! Moglie e figlio accompagnano brevemente il loro caro alla banchina del porto in attesa dell'imbarco per la Francia e il fronte occidentale.

LA GRANDE GUERRA A COLORI

STRAORDINARIE IMMAGINI RICOLORATE RIDANNO VITA AGLI ORRORI PATITI DA TUTTI I SOLDATI DURANTE LA PRIMA GUERRA MONDIALE

Quando si guardano le vecchie foto in bianco e nero, il passato sembra molto lontano. Questo è particolarmente evidente soprattutto con le fotografie della prima guerra mondiale. Soldiershop, nel centenario della Grande Guerra vi offre una biblioteca unica e innovativa con questa serie di foto colorate della prima guerra mondiale.

Le immagini non trattano solo le importanti battaglie della guerra, ma anche la vita sul fronte domestico, le industrie, gli ospedali, i progressi della tecnica e delle comunicazioni...

Il progetto "Great war in colour" consiste nella accurata selezione e poi ricolorazione di alcune delle migliori immagini relative agli anni 1914-1918 provenienti da varie biblioteche e archivi del mondo.

Il nostro ringraziamento speciale va a tutte quelle diverse istituzioni, musei, biblioteche, collezioni pubbliche o private e atenei che con la loro politica aperta in materia di copyright relativa all'uso di parte delle loro collezioni ci hanno permesso l'uso di molte immagini presenti nei nostri libri realizzati specificatamente per il centenario dell'armistizio .

Diversi milioni di foto in bianco e nero esistono negli archivi mondiali di eventi relativi alla prima guerra mondiale, una miriade di "scatti" raccolti su tutti i lati del fronte, per lo più da fotografi rimasti anonimi. La maggior parte di queste foto mostrano gli eventi devastanti della Grande Guerra, ma anche la vita di tutti i giorni nelle trincee e nelle linee di prossimità e nelle retrovie. Ed ancora negli ospedali, nelle cucine nelle fabbriche impegnate nello sforzo bellico.

Da allora, sono stati pubblicati moltissimi libri di fotografie in bianco e nero della guerra, in quanto tutte le nazioni, coinvolte e no, si sono sforzate di comprendere la scala, la carneficina e tutte le terribile complicazioni provocate dalla "terribile guerra del XX secolo".

Per celebrare il centenario dello scoppio della guerra, i nostri libri riuniscono tutte queste straordinarie e ricolorate immagini della WW1.

Il volume rappresenta l'opera di diversi artisti e collaboratori di Soldiershop, ma si basa soprattutto sul lavoro dei due principali autori: Luca Cristini e Joel Bellviure. Hanno altresì collaborato a questo volume Roberto Costanzo e Anna Cristini.

I libri della serie WW1 presentano tutto il testo e le note didascaliche in lingua inglese e italiana.

◄ Two ANZAC soldier Fighting in the Middle East, both are men of 5th Essex Brigade - one of the Kitchener brigades
Due soldati ANZAC destinati al fronte del medio oriente, entrambi della V Essex Brigate organizzata a suo tempo da Kitchener.

THE BRITISH ARMY DURING WORLD WAR 1

The **British Army during WW1** was made up exclusively of volunteers—as opposed to conscripts—at the beginning of the conflict. Furthermore, the British Army was considerably smaller than its French and German armies.

During World War I, there were almost three distinct British forces. The "first" army was the small volunteer force of about 400,000 soldiers. Of this army, over half were engaged overseas to garrison the British Empire. This first army were the sum of the Regular Army and reservists in the Territorial Force (TF). Together, they formed the British Expeditionary Force (BEF), which was formed for service in France and became known as the Old Contemptibles. The 'second' army was Kitchener's Army, formed from the volunteers in 1914–1915 destined to go into action at the Battle of the Somme. The 'third' was formed after the introduction of a first conscription, as in all the other nations, in January 1916. So at the end of the war in 1918, the British Army had reached its maximum strength of 4,000,000 men and could field over 70 divisions. The vast majority of the British Army fought in the main theatre of war on the Western Front in France and Belgium against the German Empire. Some units were engaged in Italy and Salonika against Austria-Hungary and the Bulgarian Army, while other units fought in the Middle East, Africa and Mesopotamia—mainly against the Ottoman Empire. When the war ended in November 1918, British Army casualties, as the result of enemy action and disease, were recorded as 680,000 dead and missing, with another 1,650,000 wounded. The rush to demobilize at the end of the conflict substantially decreased the strength of the British Army, from its peak strength of 4,000,000 men in 1918 to 370,000 men by 1920.

ORGANIZATION

At the outbreak of the war in August 1914, the British regular army was a small professional force. It consisted of about 250,000 regular troops organised in four regiments of Guards (Grenadier, with 3 Battalions; Coldstream, with 3 Battalions; Scots, with 2 Battalions; Irish with 1 Battalion), 68 regiments of the line and the Rifle Brigade (despite its name, this was an infantry regiment), 31 cavalry regiments, artillery and other support arms. Of this small army, almost half was stationed overseas in garrisons throughout the British Empire. The Royal Flying Corps was part of the British Army until 1918. At the outbreak of the war, it consisted of a total of 84 aircraft. The regulars and reserves of British army totaled a mobilized force of almost 700,000 men, although only 150,000 men were immediately available to be formed into the British Expeditionary Force (BEF) that was sent to the continent. For understand the difference, the French Army in 1914 mobilized 1,650,000 troops and 62 infantry divisions, while the German Army mobilized 1,850,000 troops and 87 infantry divisions!

◀ Highland Territorials soldiers in a trench, late 1916.
Soldati di un corpo territoriale degli Higlander in trincea. Tardo 1916

THE BRITISH COMMANDERS

In august 1914 the first Commander in Chief of the BEF was Field Marshal John French. We remember here that his last active command had been the cavalry division in the Second Boer War... The other commanders of the British Corps in 1914 was Douglas Haig (1st corps), the Lieutenant General James Grierson (2nd corps) . After the failed offensive at the Battle of Loos in 1915, French was replaced as commander of the BEF by Haig, who remained in command for the rest of the war. He became most famous for his role as its commander during the battle of the Somme, the battle of Passchendaele, and the Hundred Days Offensive, the series of victories leading to the German surrender in 1918. As substitute of the command of 1st corps Haig call the General Charles Carmichael Monro, who in turn was succeeded by General Henry Horne in September 1916.

In 1914, General Edmund Allenby was commander of the Cavalry Division and later the Cavalry Corps in the BEF. Allenby was replaced as Third Army commander by General Julian Byng, who began later the war as commander of the 3rd Cavalry Division. On the Macedonian front, General George Milne commanded the British Salonika Army, and General Ian Hamilton commanded the allied army during the Gallipoli Campaign. As several of his colleagues he had previously seen service in the First Boer War, the Sudan campaign, and the Second Boer War.

THE BRITISH EMPIRE IN THE FIRST WORLD WAR

In 1914 the British Government knew it's armed forces were too small to take on the might of the Central Powers. So the British Empire was called to arms and volunteers from Australia, Canada, New Zealand, Newfoundland and the Union of South Africa flocked to the aid of the mother country, joined by soldiers from other African colonies and the Indian Army with it's Gurkhas from Nepal. The immense sacrifices made by the men of British Empire on the battlefields of Europe echo across the intervening years as part of a proud Commonwealth shared history.

At Gallipoli, Neuve Chapelle, Vimy Ridge, the Somme and Ypres the graves of the fallen are powerful reminders of our debt to the Empire.

AUSTRALIA

In Australia, the outbreak of World War I was greeted with considerable enthusiasm. The first campaign that Australians were involved in was in German New Guinea after a hastily raised force known as the Australian Naval and Military Expeditionary Force was dispatched from Australia to seize German possessions in the Pacific in September 1914. At the same time an expeditionary force, of about 20,000 men and known as the First Australian Imperial Force (AIF), was raised for service overseas. These men arrived as first step in Egypt, where they were initially used to defend the Suez Canal. In early 1915, however, it was decided to carry out the famous amphibious landing on the Gallipoli peninsula with the goal of opening up a second front and securing the passage of the Dardanelles. The Australians and New Zealanders, grouped together as the Australian and New Zealand Army Corps (ANZAC), went ashore on 25 April 1915 and for the next eight months the Anzacs, alongside their British, French and other allies, fought a costly and ultimately unsuccessful campaign against the Turks. After this disaster the soldiers returned to Egypt, where the AIF was expanded. In early 1916 it was decided that the infantry divisions would be sent to France, where they took part in many of the major battles fought on the Western Front. Most of the light horse units remained in the Middle East until the end of the war, carrying out further operations against the Turks in Egypt and Palestine. The Australian involvement of the entire war cost more than 60,000 Australian lives and many more were left unable to work as a result of their injuries.

NEW ZEALAND

The WW1 history of New Zealand began in August 1914 when Great Britain declared war on Germany at the start of the First World War, the New Zealand government followed without hesitation, despite its geographic isolation and small population. The total number of New Zealand troops and nurses to serve overseas in 1914–18, excluding those in British and other Dominion

◀ Tank Corp's mascot, 'Stunter', and his officer, France, during World War I. Mascots were kept by many groups of soldiers. Often they were strays which were picked up on the move and given a temporary home. They could be used to alleviated the boredom, tension and impersonality of the war.

La mascotte dei carristi scozzesi "Stunter", e il suo ufficiale, in Francia, nel 1916 circa. Le mascotte erano tenute da molti corpi militari inglesi. Spesso erano randagi trovati per caso. Venivano usati per alleviare la noia, la tensione e l'impersonalità della guerra.

forces, was considerable, about 100,000, from a population of just over a million. Forty-two per-cent of men of military age served in the New Zealand Expeditionary Force, fighting in the Gal-lipoli Campaign and on the Western Front. 16,700 New Zealanders were killed and 41,317 were wounded during the war – a 58 percent casualty rate. One of the greatest of the entire war! The First World War saw Maori soldiers serve for the first time in a major conflict with the New Zealand Army for a total of about 3.000 men in the entire conflict. A Maori contingent took part in the Gallipoli Campaign, and later served with distinction on the Western Front.

CANADA

The British declaration of war of 1914 automatically brought Canada into the war, because of Cana-da's legal status as a British dominion which left foreign policy decisions in the hands of the British parliament. The Militia was not mobilized and instead an independent Canadian Expeditionary Force was immediately raised. Canada's sacrifices and contributions to the Great War changed its history and enabled it to become more independent, while also opening a deep rift between the French and English-speaking populations. For the first time in Canadian military history, Canadian forces fought as a distinct unit, first under a British commander but later in the war under a Cana-dian-born commander. The most important battles of Canadian military achievement during the Great War came during the Somme, Vimy, and Passchendaele battles and what later became known as "Canada's Hundred Days". Canada's total casualties stood at the end of the war at about 70,000 killed and 250,000 wounded, out of an expeditionary force of 600,000 people mobilized (39% of mobilized were casualties). Canadian support was one of the most important of their Motherland.

INDIAN ARMY DURING WORLD WAR I

The **Indian Army during World War I** was composed by a large number men, about one million, composed into divisions and independent brigades in all the world fronts: Europe, Mediterranean and the Middle East theatres of war in World War I. The Indian army loss in WW1 about 75,000 died and another 67,000 wounded. The Indian soldiers fought against the German Empire in German East Africa and on the Western Front, in Egypt, Gallipoli and Mesopotamia against the Ottoman Empire. While some divisions were sent overseas others had to remain in India guarding the North West Frontier and on internal security and training duties.

ORGANISATION OF THE ARMY

In 1914, the Indian Army was one of the two largest volunteer armies in the world with a total strength of about 250,000 men. For sample we remember that the British Army had a strength of the same number, 247,000 regular volunteers at the outbreak of the war, and at the end of the war it contained 548,311 men. It was regularly called upon to deal with incursions and raids on the North West Frontier and to provide garrison forces for the British Empire in all the world, principally in Egypt, Singapore and China. The Indian field force was divided into two armies: The Northern Army which stretched from the North-West Frontier to Bengal with five divisions and three brigades under command and the Southern Army which stretched from Baluchistan to southern India and it in turn had four di-visions under command and two formations outside the subcontinent. This two armies contained 39 cavalry regiments, 138 infantry battalions (including 20 Gurkha), a Corps of Guides, three sapper regi-ments and 12 mountain artillery batteries. The nine divisions formed by these reforms each consisted of one cavalry and three infantry brigades. The cavalry brigade had one British and two Indian regi-ments while the infantry brigades consisted of one British and three Indian battalions. Indian Army battalions were smaller than the British battalions, consisting of 30 officers and about 750 troops as compared to the British 29 officers and 977 other ranks. To avoid some problems, Indian battalions were often segregated, with companies of different tribes, castes or religions. Additional troops attached to the headquarters of each division included a cavalry regiment, a pioneer battalion and artillery provided by the British Royal Field Artillery. Each division had about 13,000 men on strength. In addition to the regular Indian Army, the armies of the Indian minor States and regiments of the Auxiliary Force (European volunteers) could also be called upon to assist in an emergency. The Princely States (Indian minor states) formed the Imperial Service Brigades and in 1914, they furnished about 23,000 men in 20 cavalry regiments and 14 infantry battalions. The Auxiliary force could field another 40,000 men in 11 regiments of horse and 42 volunteer infantry battalions. The field force headquarters was located in Delhi, India. In 1914, the Commander–in–Chief was General Sir Beauchamp Duff of the Indian Army, and the Chief of the General Staff was Lieutenant General Sir Percy Lake of the British Army, both English men obviously! Each Indian battalion was staffed by 13 officers from the British Army in India and 17 officers from the Indian Army. As the war intensified and officer casualties mounted, the ability to replace casualties with officers of British origin became extremely difficult and, as *extrema ratio* in some occasions they were selected for officer training at the Royal Military College. During the course of the Great war over 800,000 men volunteered for the army and more than 400,000 volunteered for non-combatant roles. In total almost 1.3 million men had volunteered for service in the five years of the war! The British army used also Indian child soldiers, some as young as 10 years old, in the war. The Indian Army formed and dispatched a total of seven expeditionary forces overseas during World War I.

▲ ANZAC men in pose for a shot in the Egyptian desert. 1916 about
Soldati del corpo di spedizione australiano e neozelandese in posa per una foto ricordo in mezzo al deserto, 1916 circa.

L'ESERCITO BRITANNICO NELLA GRANDE GUERRA

La Grande Guerra si rilevò uno dei teatri bellici più devastanti e luttuosi dell'intera storia militare inglese. Alla fine del conflitto l'impero britannico lasciò sul terreno circa ottocentomila morti e oltre due milioni di feriti. Nella prima parte della guerra, la Gran Bretagna, che non aveva la coscrizione obbligatoria, mandò al fronte un piccolo ma ben addestrato contingente che venne coinvolto nelle principali battaglie sul continente tra cui la cruenta e logorante Battaglia della Somme. L'avanzamento nelle tecnologie portò convince i britannici fra i primi ad usare i carri armati, ed il progredire anche nel progetto dei velivoli, alla costituzione del prestigioso Royal Flying Corps, che sarà decisivo nelle future battaglie. La guerra di trincea fu tuttavia la strategia dominante del fronte occidentale, e l'uso dei gas chimici portò alla devastazione più totale anche fra le fila dei tommies. Quando nel 1914 scoppiò la Prima guerra mondiale, l'esercito inglese inviò un corpo di spedizione denominato BEF (British Expeditionary Force) in Francia e Belgio per impedire o contrastare l'occupazione di quei territori da parte delle truppe germaniche. Contemporaneamente, su idea del capo dell'ammiragliato, Sir W.Churchill venne creato il Mediterranean Expeditionary Force in Egitto successivamente inviato a Gallipoli nel tentativo fallito di riprendere Costantinopoli ed assicurare le vie navali verso la Russia. Dopo lilò fallimento di tale operazione e la ritirata da Gallipoli quasi 400.000 uomini in 13 divisioni del Mediterranean Expeditionary Force e le forze in Egitto formarono una riserva strategica chiamata Egyptian Expeditionary Force che prese parte a tutte le campagne in Palestina e Mesopotamia e ad operare la difesa del Canale di Suez. Fronte occidentale a parte, i soldati inglesi passarono all'offensiva in tutti gli altri teatri, specialmente in quelli coloniali. Immediatamente la Gran Bretagna invase e occupò la maggior parte delle colonie d'oltremare della Germania in Africa. Nel Pacifico, l'Australia e la Nuova Zelanda occuparono rispettivamente la Nuova Guinea tedesca e Samoa. Mentre i piani per una divisione post-bellica dell'impero ottomano, che si schierò in guerra a fianco della Germania, furono segretamente redatti dalla Gran Bretagna e dalla Francia nel quadro dell'accordo Sykes-Picot del 1916. La dichiarazione di guerra britannica contro la Germania ei suoi alleati coinvolse immediatamente le fedeli colonie e i Domini che fornirono preziosi aiuti in termini di personale militare, sostegno finanziario e materiali. Oltre 2,5 milioni di uomini dell'impero britannico serviranno per la corona britannica durante i cinque anni del conflitto. Il contributo di sangue delle truppe australiane e neozelandesi durante la Campagna di Gallipoli del 1915 contro l'Impero Ottomano, fu talmente elevato da sollevare in patria un grande impatto sulla coscienza nazionale e segnarono un momento decisivo nel passaggio dell'Australia e della Nuova Zelanda da colonie a nazioni completamente autonome. I paesi continuano ancor 'oggi a commemorare questi eventi in occasione dell'*ANZAC Day*. I canadesi dal canto loro, ottennero la vittoria nella battaglia del crinale di Vimy con risultati simili a quelli dell'ANZAC. Alla fine del conflitto, a seguito dei trattati di Versailles firmato nel 1919, l'impero britannico, incamerando gran parte delle ex colonie tedesche, raggiunse l'apice delle sue dimensioni con l'acquisizione di 4.700.000 km² di territorio e 13 milioni di nuovi soggetti. Fra le nuove colonie

◄ A serious news...a famous WW1 British postcards with a very young boys in military uniform...
"Una notizia seria". famosa cartolina postale che mostra un bambino vestito da ufficiale mentre studia un giornale..

ricordiamo la Palestina, la Transgiordania, l'Iraq, parti del Camerun e del Togo e il controllo di Tanganica. Gli stessi Domini accrebbero le loro dimensioni: l'Unione Sudafricana acquisì il Sud-Africa occidentale (l'attuale Namibia), l'Australia la Nuova Guinea tedesca, la Nuova Zelanda la Samoa Occidentale.

GLI ESERCITI DEI DOMINI IMPERIALI BRITANNICI

CANADA

Il Canada partecipò attivamente e almeno all'inizio con entusiasmo alla prima guerra mondiale, schierandosi a fianco delle nazioni dell'Intesa nel 1914. La data monumento dello sforzo canadese nella prima guerra mondiale è ricordato nella battaglia di Vimy Ridge del 9 aprile 1917, presso il Passo di Calais in Francia, nella quale le truppe canadesi riuscirono, dopo 3 giorni di assedio, a conquistare una collina fortificata tedesca che aveva eroicamente resistito a numerosi precedenti attacchi britannici e francesi. Battaglie come quelle di Vimy, insieme al glorioso impegno della forza aerea canadese, nell'ambito della quale si distinsero singoli aviatori come William Barker e Billy Bishop, contribuirono a definire una nuova identità al paese nordamericano. La partecipazione al conflitto pertanto contribuì a diffondere nell'opinione pubblica interna un maggiore spirito nazionalistico, cosa del resto assai diffusa e presente anche in tutte le altre nazioni dei domini britannici.

AUSTRALIA

Negli anni della Prima Guerra Mondiale il numero di soldati che l'Australia poteva fornire non era abbastanza vasto per poter dare un suo contributo al conflitto per questa ragione al termine del loro addestramento i leader dello stato maggiore britannico proposero di unire le forze armate australiane con quelle neozelandesi, formando l'Australian and New Zealand Army Corps (ANZAC). L'Australia tuttavia il 15 agosto 1914 fornì anche un secondo corpo di spedizione, l'Australian Imperial Force che contava 20.000 soldati obbligati a giurare fedeltà alla corona britannica e sotto il comando dei generali inglesi. Una volta giunte in Egitto, le truppe australiane e neozelandesi fortemente legate alla loro provenienza, dettero prova di "indisciplina" portando alla formazione del mito nazionale. Quest'ultimo fu maggiormente enfatizzato nel 1915 dalla tragica battaglia a Gallipoli dove persero la vita circa 8.000 giovani australiani. Questo episodio ben mameggiato dai media del tempo contribuì non poco a creare la leggenda del soldato australiano dotato di particolari doti di coraggio e di sopravvivenza. Nel 1916-1917, per l'ANZAC fu la volta del fronte occidentale dove anxhe subirono ingenti perdite: quasi 40.000 uomini nei due anni. Alla fine del conflitto, la sola Australia lamentò circa 60.000 morti e 150.000 feriti e invalidi su una popolazione complessiva di circa 5 milioni di abitanti. Circa i due terzi dei combattenti rimasero uccisi o feriti e la maggior parte di questi erano volontari, una cifra record nella prima guerra mondiale.

NUOVA ZELANDA

La Nuova Zelanda dichiarò guerra all'Impero tedesco il 5 agosto 1914, imitando il Regno Unito e gli altri dominions; il governo neozelandese si impegnò fin da principio nelle ostilità, prima inviando un piccolo distaccamento ad occupare la colonia tedesca di Samoa il 29 agosto 1914, e poi offrendo al Regno Unito un contingente di circa 9.000 volontari (divisi in una brigata di fanteria ed una di cavalleria) per il servizio oltremare. La "New Zealand Expeditionary Force" questo è il nome assegnato a questo primo contingente, sbarcò in Egitto il 3 dicembre 1914, sotto il comando del generale Alexander Godley. In Egitto avvenne poi quanto scritto sopra a proposito del contingente australiano, poiché entrambe le forze del Pacifico erano troppo piccole per dare vita ad una divisione autonoma, venne creato il famoso "Australian and New Zealand Army Corps" o ANZAC: in particolare, la brigata di fanteria venne inquadrata con la 4ª Brigata fanteria australiana nella New Zealand and Australian Division, mentre la brigata montata fu integrata nella cavalleria del corpo. Il 25 aprile 1915, l'ANZAC sbarcò sulla penisola di Gallipoli, prendendo così parte alla campagna dei Dardanelli contro l'Impero ottomano; praticamente isolate dal resto del contingente alleato, sbarcato più a sud, le forze australiane e neozelandesi tennero la precaria posizione per molti mesi, venendo impegnate in sanguinosi scontri con le forze ottomane. Benché composto da truppe di nuova formazione e praticamente prive di esperienza bellica, l'ANZAC si distinse nei combattimenti, dimostrandosi il miglior contingente delle forze alleate impiegate nella campagna; le truppe alleate vennero poi ritirate dalla penisola ai primi di gennaio del 1916: il contingente neozelandese uscì semidistrutto dalla inconcludente campagna, con la perdita di quasi il 90% degli effettivi tra morti e feriti. Le truppe neozelandesi insieme a quelle australiane vennero ritirate in Egitto per essere riorganizzate: l'arrivo di nuovi reparti dalla madrepatria (dove il 1º agosto 1916 venne introdotta, non senza polemiche, la coscrizione obbligatoria) rese possibile la creazione di un'intera divisione neozelandese che venne inviata sul fronte occidentale nell'aprile del 1916. Qui le truppe neozelandesi si batterono con onore fino alla fine delle ostilità, distinguendosi in particolare durante le battaglie di Messines, di Passchendaele, e nell'offensiva dei cento giorni. Le unità a cavallo rimasero invece in Egitto dove, inquadrate insieme alle omologhe unità australiane, vennero impiegate nella campagna del Sinai e della Palestina fino all'ottobre del 1918. Su una popolazione di poco più di un milione di abitanti, i neozelandesi arruolarono nel corso della prima guerra mondiale circa 120.000 soldati quasi tutti inviati oltreoceano; le perdite ammontarono a 18.500 morti e 50.000 feriti.

INDIA
Prima dello scoppio della Grande Guerra, l'Esercito dell'India britannica contava 150.000 soldati; al novembre del 1918 il numero degli effettivi era salito a quasi 600.000. Dopo le riforme di Kitchener, l'Esercito Indiano venne sempre impiegato a fianco dell'Esercito britannico, ancorché peggio equipaggiato. Una divisione consisteva di tre brigate, divise ciascuna in quattro battaglioni, tre britannici e uno indiano. Prima della guerra, il Governatorato indiano aveva stabilito che la colonia poteva permettersi di fornire due divisioni di fanteria e una brigata di cavalleria nel caso di una guerra europea. Una mobilitazione maggiore avrebbe messo a rischio la sicurezza nazionale della colonia. Si formarono quindi, nell'ambito di detti limiti i primi corpi di spedizione Indiani che furono schierati sul fronte occidentale già nel 1914. Le alte perdite iniziali del conflitto, soprattutto fra gli ufficiali misero però a rischio tale partecipazione nei fatti esigua. Tuttavia, grazie al fatto che i temuti disordini nel subcontinente indiano non ebbero mai luogo, l'India poté garantire molte altre divisioni che vennero impiegate in servizio attivo per tutto il corso della guerra. Nella prima guerra mondiale l'Esercito Indiano svolse un intenso servizio effettivo, che incluse tra l'altro: Fronte occidentale, la Battaglia di Gallipoli, la Campagna del Sinai e della Palestina e della Mesopotamia ed infine l'Africa Orientale, compresa la Battaglia di Tanga. Il sacrificio di sangue degli indiani assommò a 43.000 soldati caduti, mentre 65.000 rimasero feriti. Nella guerra vennero inoltre schierate anche le cosiddette truppe al servizio dell'Impero (*Imperial Service Troops*), fornite da diversi Principati indiani autonomi. Furono in tutto circa 21.000 uomini, perlopiù provenienti dai Sikh del Punjab e dai Rajput del Rajputana (come il Corpo dei Cammellieri di Bikaner o i lancieri di Jodhpur. Queste unità giocarono un ruolo di primo piano nella Campagna del Sinai e della Palestina.

THE ENGLISH MEN

GLI INGLESI

◄ 1914 A British soldier with his wife and daughter before the beggining of the war.

1914 Come in tutte le nazioni, anche fra gli inglesi era di moda fare un'ultima foto ricordo con la famiglia prima di partire.

1914 THE TOMMIES GO TO THE WAR

1914 TUONANO I CANNONI D'AGOSTO

◄ **1914** young recruits just enrolled in the army pose for their first strong image

1914 Giovani reclute inglese appena arruolate nell'esercito posano per la loro prima "forte" immagine..

▼ **1917** Two members of the Women's Army Auxiliary Corps, France, during World War I. The two women in this image seem happy and relaxed. They are laughing and joking with each other and seem to share a good rapport with each other. They find German helmets useful substitutes for market bags..

1917 due membri del corpo ausiliario femminile dell'esercito in Francia. Le due dinne appaiono molto rilassate ed anche divertite nella foto. esse portano ironicamente degli elmetti tedeschi alla stregua di borse della spesa.

◄ **1914** A classical Tommy in his kaki uniform.

1914 la classica tenuta color kaki indosatta dall'esercito inglese nel corso di tutta la guerra.

▼ **1916** A line of soldiers of the Gordon Highlanders leaving its camp to the frontline while a line of British soldiers -most likely cavalry- watch as the troops march past along the road, 1916. They were the most reputed Scottish units in the war.

1916 Marcia di un battaglione di Gordon Highlanders verso il fronte sotto lo sguardo curioso di truppe inglesi di cavalleria.

☞ Next pages: **1917** British gun going to its position, Ypres, Belgium. This shows a heavy artillery gun being transported along a road towards the Front.

1917 Gigantesco cannone inglese prende posizione nella zona di Ypres nelle Fiandre (Belgio)

1916 THE TERRIFIC GAS WAR

1916 IL TERRIBILE GAS APPARE SUI CAMPI DI BATTAGLIA

◄ ▼ **1916** British Vickers machine gun crew wearing PH-type anti-gas masks, near Ovillers during the Battle of the Somme, July 1916. These pictures were purely promotional and do not depict an actual gas attack, since a soldier -in many versions cropped- can be seen behind without any mask. These were published as RPPCs (Real Photo Postcards) during the war as promotional material; many originals were colourised with watercolour.

1916 Gruppi di mitraglieri e soldati britannici, dotati di arma Vickers e tutti forniti di opportune maschere a gas di tipo diverso.

☞ Next pages: **1916** British soldiers arriving in a village. They are surrounded by women and children. One soldier has lifted a young girl onto his bicycle. They are all walking along a muddy road through the village. The buildings in the distance appear to be untouched by bombing or shelling. The arrival of allied troops in a village was cause for great excitement. Once troops entered a village they were often housed with local families. This was a welcome opportunity for rest and a diversion for the locals.

1916 l'arrivo di truppe britanniche in un villaggio del nord della Francia, coi soldati circondati dall'entusiasmo della popolazione locale, soprattutto donne e bambini.

La Fessée!

1914-1918 SPORT & IRONY
1914-1918 LO SPORT E L'IRONIA

◄ **1914** Allegorical image of the two British-Frank allies intent on spanking (la fessée) to the evil German brat.

1914 Immagine allegotica dei due alleati franco britannici intenti a sculacciare (la fessée) il perfido fantaccino tedesco.

▼ **1916** Mule in a limber team collapses after being hit by a shell splinter near the village of Rémy, during the Battle of the Drocourt-Quéant Line, part of The Hundred Days Offensive. This battle ended with the German forces withdrawing 64 km to the Hindenburg Line, which would be broken shortly after the events.

1916 Un mula adibito al traino d'artiglieria stramazza al suolo sfinito dalla fatica della guerra. La scena avviene nei dintorni del vollaggio di Remy durante la battaglia di Drocourt-Quéant.

◄ **1917** Walter Daniel John Tull (28 April 1888 – 25 March 1918) was an English professional footballer. He was commissioned as a Second Lieutenant on 30 May 1917, after receiving many decorations. Tull was the first black officer from the British Army to lead troops. He returned to France in 1918, and was killed in action on 25 March during the Spring Offensive.

1917 Walter Daniel John Tull (1888-1918) fu un famoso giocatore di calcio dei suoi tempi. Durante la guerra egli divenne il primo ufficiale di colore dell'esercito britannico. Colpito e ucciso in azione in Francia il 25 maggio 1918 durante un azione dell'offensiva di primavera.

▼ **1918** WAACs with English, Scottish, and ANZAC convalescent soldiers playing basketball at Étaples, 1 May 1918.

1918 Ausiliarie femminili, uomini dell'ANZAC e scozzesi convalescenti giocano tutti insieme a basket nei dintorni di Etaples nel nord della Francia.

☞ Next pages: **1917** A squadron troop of cavalry crossing a stream in France near st. Floris. photographer H.D.Girdwood

1917 Uno squadrone di cavalleria inglese in perlustrazione attraversa un ruscello nei pressi di San Floris in Francia. Foto del noto corrispondente di guerra H.D.Girdwood.

THE LIFE OF THE SOLDIERS
LA VITA DEI SOLDATI

◄ **1917** John (Jack) Elkins - A Soldiers Tale. A record war shot...

1917 Ispirato scatto del soldato John (Jaxk) Elkins.

▼ **1917** "Wild Eye", the Souvenir King. The private John "Barney" Hines of the Australian 45th Battalion surrounded by German equipment he looted during the Battle of Polygon Wood in September 1917. He is counting money stolen from German POWs, wearing a German Army field cap and sitting amidst German weapons and personal equipment.

1917 Il tesoretto tedesco ritrovato da uno stupefatto soldato australiano, il soldato semplice John Barney..

☞ Next pages: **1917** British Army chaplain conducts a service from the cockpit of an aeroplane, in north of France, during World War I

1917 Curiosa immagine che mostra una messa la campo, in cui il cappellano militare utilizza la carlinga del grande aereo da bombardamento alla stregua di un pulpito.

WW1 THE RED CROSS SERVICE

INFERMIERE E SERVIZI SANITARI

◀ **1917** A smiling red- cross nurse .. Silent film actress June Caprice wearing a Red Cross nurses uniform as a promotion for buying WWI Liberty Loan Bonds

1917 Una sorridente crocerossina… In realtà si tratta di una diva del cinema muto, June Caprice che prestò il suo viso ad una campagna di raccolti fondi per la croce rossa durante la prima guerra mondiale.

▼ **1917** Wounded soldiers being carried aboard a boat on stretchers. Two women, possibly nurses, are standing on the quayside talking to a soldier and watching the men going up the gangplank. It is difficult to say from this photograph how badly wounded the men being carried aboard are. They both look conscious and the one nearest the quayside appears to be watching all this activity with interest. Scenes such as this were commonly used as propaganda, intended to provide reassurance to those at home.

1917 Soldati feriti vengono trasportati all'interno di una nave ospedale sotto lo sguardo attento di due crocerossine intente a parlare con un soldato di guardia.

THE BRITISH "RED BARON"

IL BARONE ROSSO INGLESE

◄ **1918** Major James McCudden in front of his No. 60 Squadron RAF Vickers FB16 biplane, c. 1918. In August 1914, one month after the war had started, he travelled to France and operated as a reconnaissance unit, starting to fly as an observer. Deeper into 1915, he managed to act as an aerial gunner. On 21 January 1916 McCudden was awarded the Croix de Guerre for gallantry, received in person by General Joffre. He achieved a total of 57 aerial victories.

1918 Il maggiore James McCudden uno degli assi dell'aviazione britannica con all'attivo ben 57 vittorie aeree.

▼ **1918** British officer and his dog look at James McCudden's tomb in the Wavans War Cemetery, Pas de Calais, 13 July 1918. McCudden's intention was to surpass the Red Baron, who had been killed in action few months before he was sent to France. McCudden's remains would be buried together around three dozen graves, in the Pas de Calais, France.

1918 Un ufficiale inglese in compagnia del suo cane prega sulla tomba del super asso dell'aviazione inglese James McCudden, abbattuto sui cieli di Calais il 13 luglio 1918.

☞ Next pages: **1917** 4th East Lancashire Regiment in the trenches at Nieuport Bains, the extreme left of the line. The sergeant in the foreground is watching the German line in a periscope fixed on his bayonet.

1917 Uomini del 4° Lancashire regiment in una trincea nei pressi di Nieuport bains. Il sergente nel messo dell'immagine osserva le linee nemiche attraverso un periscopio di fortuna posto sulla baionetta.

1916 THE USEFUL MILITARY TRANSPORTS

L'IMPORTANZA DI UNA BUONA SUSSISTENZA.

◄ **1916** Loading up a supply column aire in North France. photographer H.D.Girdwood

1916 Carico di una colonna di autocarri con materiale per la forza aerea. Nord della francia.

▼ **1916** Supply column waiting to load at a railway station Aire, France

1916 Colonna di carri della sussistenza in attesa di caricare una stazione aerea. Nord della Francia.

☞ Next pages: **1917** Two woman driver of the Women auxiliary army corps on his Red Cross truck in a destroyed French village.

1917 due donne ausiliarie della croce rossa inglese alla guida di un'autoambulanza in un villaggio francese.

PRESENTED
TO

BY
SUTTON COLDFIELD
AND DISTRICT

◄ **1916** Party of Royal Irish Rifles in a communication trench on the first day of the Battle of the Somme, 1 July 1916.

1916 Soldati del Royal Irish Rifle in trincea il primo giorno della battaglia della Somme.

◄ **1917** Lancashire Fusiliers in a flooded communication trench opposite Messines, near Ploeg-steert Wood, Belgium, in January 1917.

1917 Fucilieri del Lancashire regiment in una trincea inondata a Messines in Belgio.

▼ **1918** British men around one of the first tanks of history… All these young men have already passed; a reflection of the distance of time.

1918 Soldati inglesi attorno ad un gigantesco carro armato, oggi a distanza di tempo fa riflettere pensare che tutti gli uomini di questa immagine sono già tutti morti

◄ **1917** Soldier's comrades watching him as he sleeps, Thievpal, France, Soldiers are standing in a very deep, narrow trench, the walls of which are entirely lined with sandbags. At the far end of the trench a line of soldiers are squashed up looking over each others' shoulders at the soldier asleep.

1917 soldato sfinito cade nelle braccia di Morfeo in un sonno ristoratore sotto lo sguardo dei suoi camerati.

◄ **1918** A Lewis gun position in a trench held by 15th Battalion, Royal Scots, probably near Croissilles.

1918 una postazione di mitragliatrice Lewis gun tenuta da truppe scozzesi a Crossilles.

▼ **1916** Royal Highlanders of Canada soldier cleaning his Short Lee Enfield rifle, June, 1916.

1916 Royal Highlanders canadese intento a pulire il suo Lee-Enfield.

☞ Next pages: **1917** Vickers machine gun in action during the terrible battle of Passchendaele, fought in the September 1917

1917 Una mitragliatrice Vickers in azione con il suo equipaggio durante la terribile battaglia di Passchendaele combattuta nel settembre del 1917.

◄ **1918** Six "Tommies" from the Royal Engineers posing over a temporary bridge in the Somme River, c. 1918. Many are wearing the leather jerkin, jackets issued by the British Army in order to protect against the cold and mud. The Royal Engineers were, on the other hand, a branch of the British Army with a centenary history that played a major role during World War I.

1918 Sei soldati del genio britannico posano sul malfermo ponte gettato sul fiume Somme. Il genio britannico vantava già secoli di storia e giocò un ruolo importante durante la grande guerra.

▼ **1918** The fox cub mascot of No. 32 Squadron RAF in a S.E.5 plane, at Humières Aerodrome, St. Pol, France, 5 May 1918. The Royal Flying Corps (RFC) was the air branch of the British Army during World War One, until April 1, 1918, when the Royal Naval Air Service and the RFC united to form the RAF.

1918 La mascotte del 32° squadrone RAF all'aeroporto militare di San Pol in Francia

◄ **1917** Two officers and soldiers of the Australian Medical Corps at an advanced YMCA canteen with a shelter near Wytschaete, Belgium, 11th August 1917. This picture was taken during the Third Battle of Ypres, better known as the Battle of Passchendaele.

1917 Due ufficiali e soldati del corpo medico australiano a Wytschaete Belgio. Terza battaglia di Ypres.

◄ **1918** A Lee-Enfield .303 rifle cartridge, compared with a *tank gewehr* one. The Lee-Enfield rifle was a general weapon that was used by virtually all British infantrymen serving on the Western Front during the war.

1917 Una cartuccia del fucile inglese Lee Enfield paragonata con un proiettile anticarro.

▼ **1917** Irish Guards taking a rest between carrying duckboards, near Langemarck, 10 October 1917. Duckboards were used to line the bottom of trenches on the Western Front, as these were regularly flooded, and mud and water would lie in the trenches for months on end.

1917 Guardie irlandesi in un attimo di pausa vicino alla località di Langenmarck nelle Fiandre.

◄ **1918** A Caquot kite observation balloon from the Royal Air Force in Gosnay, Pas-de-Calais, 2 May 1918. The British airships were only partly rigid, at the front and the back, while the German zeppelins were completely rigid.

1918 Un pallone da osservazione Caquot della Royal Air Force a Gosnay, Pas de Calais Francia.

◄ **1917** A British officer with a German *schutzplatte*, 1917. The *schutzplatte* was a sniper mask used by the German and Austria-Hungarian Army during WWI. It provided a level of protection as armour against shrapnel.

1917 Un ufficiale inglese collauda una piastra protettiva tedesca chiamata schutzplatte.

▼ **1918** A BL 15-inch howitzer Mk. 1, fondly known as 'Granny', with a lifting mechanism to the left, being set up, Flanders, c. 1918. Artillery was an important part of the new warfare developed between 1914 and 1918. The artillery of each army would shell the enemy trenches in order to break the trench warfare and to be able to launch infantry attacks.

1918 un cannone pesante inglese 15 inch battezzato col nomignolo "Granny". Fiandre belga.

☞ Next pages: **1918** May 2, Battle of the Lys. An English officer with his crew operate an 18-pound cannon hidden in a barn near Saint-Floris.

1918 2 Maggio, battaglia del Lys. Un ufficiale inglese insieme al suo equipaggio azionano un cannone da 18 libbre nascosto in una stalla vicino Saint-Floris.

◄ **1918** English soldiers and locals with brodie helmets outside a building with the German graffiti 'Gott strafe England' (God punish England, in German), c. 1918.

1918 Soldati inglesi e bambini locali con elmetti brodie accanto ad un edificio con la scritta "Gott strafe England" (dio punisca l'Inghilterra in tedesco).

◄ **1918** Soldiers wearing leather jerkins, gloves, and high boots before starting to work in the mud of a ditch, France, c. 1918.

1918 soldati inglesi vestiti con pesanti giacche in pelle, alti stivali e guanti si preparano a ripulire la strada dal fango. Nord della Francia

▼ **1917** British soldiers -most likely from the 16th Battalion, Royal Warwickshire Regiment- in a recently retaken German line, 1917. According to some evidence only a man, the one on the back in the trench, survived the war. The brodie helmet of the same man was pierced by a bullet, as can be seen. The brodie helmet was designed in England in 1915 by John L. Brodie. Quickly it spread along the Adrian among the Allied nations, known in the U.S. the doughboy helmet. The German slang for the helmet was Salatschüssel (salad bowl).

1917 Soldati inglesi del 16° battaglione del Royal Warwickshire Regiment hanno appena preso possesso di una trincea tedesca, da loro ribattezzata "vecchia linea degli unni…"

THE EMPIRE SOLDIERS

I SOLDATI DELL'IMPERO

◄ 1914 Harry Brain, in tropical army uniform and his brother on the right. His regiment, was the Queen's Own Oxfordshire Hussars that served throughout the war in France and Belgium.

1914 Due soldati ANZAC, in realtà si tratta di due fratelli Brain, qui ritratti in tenuta coloniale del reggimento Queen's Own Oxfordshire Hussars che prese servizio in Francia e Belgio.

◄ ▼ **1916** The Prior brothers were ANZAC soldiers that fought in the Middle East and perished on the Marquette. Joseph Prior was under age when he signed up as a regular in 1915 aged 15 years and one month. He joined the 5th Essex Brigade - one of the first Kitchener brigades. At left in studio photographic pose. Below the two brothers mounted on camels near the great Egyptian pyramids.

1916 I fratelli Prior del corpo degli ANZAC in posa su un cammello nei pressi della Sfinge e delle grandi piramidi in Egitto. A sinistra uno dei due in posa da studio fotografico.

☞ Next pages: **1915** Transport of the Sappers & Miners on the march in France

1915 una colonna di trasporti del genio zappatori e minatori in marcia nel nord della Francia.

◄ **1916** Nepal gurkhas charging a trench near Merville in France

1916 Gurkhas nepalesi impegnati nell'assalto a un trincea vicino a Merville in Francia

▼ **1916** Australian soldiers from different battalions -some possibly from the 24th or 28th Battalion, 2nd Division; according to the patches- marching along a road heading to the frontline in northern France, c. 1916.

1916 Soldati australiani, probabilmente del 24à o 28° battaglione della 2a divisione in marcia. Nord della Francia.

☞ Next pages: **1916** The general Remington with Sir Partab Singh the rajah of Rutlam riding in France. Photographer H.D.Girdwood.

1916 Il generale britannico Remington a cavallo in compagnia di Partab Singh Rajah del Rutlam in un villaggio del nord della Francia. Foto di H.D.Girdwood

◄ **1915** General Sir James Willcocks and his personal staff in the garden at his headquarters in Merville France. photographer H.D.Girdwood.

1915. Il generale Sir James Willcocks ed il suo staff nel giardino del suo comando a Merville (Francia). Foto di H.D.Girdwood.

▼ **1916** Farewell dinner to General Lipsett. 2nd Infantry Canadian Brigade. June, 1916.

1916 Cena in onore del generale Lipsett della 2a brigata di fanteria canadese.

◄ **1915** 25 July, An Indian Cavy. Brigade signal troop at work in France. Officers seated in motor car at left, ruined brick tower in background. Photographer: H. D. Girdwood

1915 Soldati indiani di una brigata di cavalleria al lavoro. con gli ufficiali all'interno di un'autovettura e le rovine di un vecchio mulino sullo sfondo.

▼ **1916** Embarkation of ANZAC soldiers on HMAT ship Ajana, Melbourne, July 8, 1916,

1916 Imbarco di truppe ANZAC sulla nave HMAT Ajana dal porto di Melbourne.

◄ **1915** 28 Jul, Mounted troopers of the 29th Lancers at Linghem in France. Photo of H.D.Girdwood

1915 Colonna di soldati indiani del 29° lancieri a Linghem in Francia.

▼ **1916** Canadian soldiers in training how to shoot from a trench

1916 Soldati canadesi in addestramento al tiro da una trincea

☞ Next pages: **1916** The arrival of mail at brigade post-office in Linghem France. Photographer H.D.Girdwood

1916 L'arrivo della posta alla brigata indiana a Linghem (Francia). Foto di H.D.Girdwood

◄ **1916** Convalescent Indians sunning themselves, and others out for their march through the town and along the bracing sea front with the Pavilion Hospital in the background [Brighton, England]. Photographer: H. D. Girdwood.

1916 soldati indiani convalescenti nei pressi del padiglione ospedaliero di Brighton.

▼ **1916** A musical party of 6th Jats Indian regiment in France (near Merville). Photographer: H. D. Girdwood.

1916 Una sezione musicale di suonatori del reggimento indiano (6° Iats) a Merville in Francia

◄ **1915** 28 July, Firing line of a troop of Jodhpur Lancers in position lying behind a screen of trees. (Linghem, France). Photographer: H. D. Girdwood.

1915 Linea di fucilieri di lancieri di Jodhpur in posizione nascosti da una fila di alberi a Linghem in Francia.

▼ **1915** General Sir James Willcocks in his headquarters in Merville France. photographer H.D.Girdwood.

1915. Il generale sir James Willcocks nel giardino del suo comando a Merville (Francia). Foto di H.D.Girdwood.

☞ Next pages: **1917** Happy Canadian soldiers on his trucks after their victory at Vimy Ridge.
1917 Felici soldati canadesi sui loro camion dopo la vittoria riportata sui tedeschi a Vimy.

o·1027

◄ **1918** A Canadian Tommy soldier covered in mud returning from the front lines

1918 Un soldato canadese coperto di fango fa ritorno falla linea del fronte.

▼ **1917** Soldiers and Canadian officers posing in front of the photographer

1917 Soldati e ufficiali canadesi in posa davanti al fotografo

◄ **1918** Indian Sikh soldier with Lee–Enfield and a sword in a photo studio, 1914. One million Indian soldiers, mainly Sikh warriors, served under the yoke of the British Empire as overseas combatants, eventually reaching 120,000 casualties in 1918.

1914 Soldato indiano Sikh armato di sciabola e fucile Lee-Enfield in una foto studio all'inizio della guerra.

▼ **1916** Private Alfred Victor Momplhait,a South Australian Soldiers. Killed in action in France in July 1916

1917 Il soldato australiano Alfred Victor Momplhait. Morto in combattimento in France nel luglio 1916

1914-1918 WW1 VOLUMES ALREADY PUBLISHED OR IN WORKING
1914-1918 WW1 I LIBRI DELLA SERIE GIÀ DISPONIBILI E/O IN LAVORAZIONE

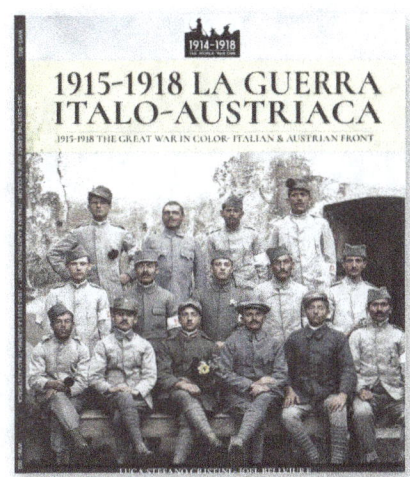 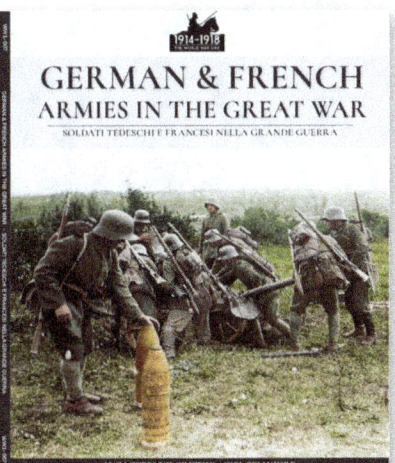 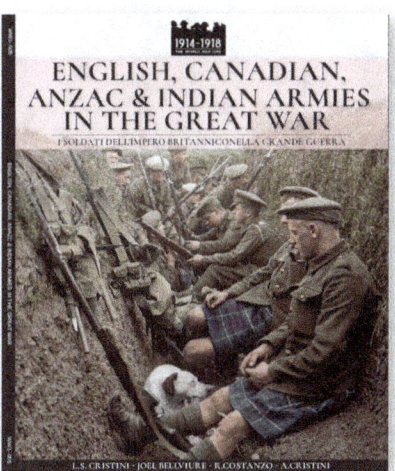

Books also in this series:

WW1-001 - 1915-1918 la Guerra Italo-Austriaca (The Great war in color -Italian & Austrian front)

WW1-002 - 1914-1918 German wartime propaganda

WW1-003 - 1915-1918 Italian pro & cons satire

WW1-004 - German & French Army in the Great War

WW1-005 - English, Canadian, ANZAC & Indian armies in the great war

◄ **1918** Australian General John Monash, GCMG, KCB, VD was one of the highest commanders of Australia, here he can be seen with a selection of his ribbons in 1918. He commanded the 4th Brigade during the Campaign of Gallipoli, to see be attached to the brand-new 3rd Division in France. His uniform is currently preserved in the Australian War Memorial.

1918 Uno fra i più famosi comandanti indigeni delle truppe australiane, il generale John Monash.

1914-1918
THE WORLD WAR ONE

BOOKS TO COLLECT